Food

BY KATHY THORNBOROUGH • ILLUSTRATIONS BY KATHLEEN PETELINSEK

PUBLISHED by The Child's World®
1980 Lookout Drive • Mankato, MN 56003-1705
800-599-READ • www.childsworld.com

ACKNOWLEDGMENTS
The Child's World®: Mary Berendes, Publishing Director
The Design Lab: Design
Jody Jensen Shaffer: Editing

PHOTO CREDITS
© ChristiTolbert/iStock.com: 19; Cloud7Days/Shutterstock.com: 5; Dan Kosmayer/Shutterstock.com: back cover, 17; Dima Sobko/Shutterstock.com: 18; EM Arts/Shutterstock.com: 8; Gam1983/Shutterstock.com: 9; Guzel Studio/Shutterstock.com: back cover, 22; HandmadePictures/Shutterstock: : 21; igor.stevanovic/Shutterstock.com: 12; indigolotos/iStock.com: 11; -lvinst-/iStock.com: 10; Kim Reinick/Shutterstock.com: 4; MaximShebeko/iStock.com: 14; MentalArt/iStock.com: 20; Nattika/Shutterstock.com: 23; panadda wattanachang: 7; Slawomir Fajer/Shutterstock.com: 16; TaneeStudio/Shutterstock.com: 13; unpict/Shutterstock.com: 15; valzan/Shutterstock.com: cover, 1, 3

COPYRIGHT © 2015 by The Child's World®
All rights reserved. No part of this book may be reproduced or utilized in any form or by any means without written permission from the publisher.

ISBN 9781626873193
LCCN 2014934499

PRINTED in the United States of America
Mankato, MN
July, 2014
PA02216

A SPECIAL THANKS TO OUR ADVISERS:
As a member of a deaf family that spans four generations, Kim Bianco Majeri lives, works, and plays amongst the deaf community.

Carmine L. Vozzolo is an educator of children who are deaf and hard of hearing, as well as their families.

NOTE TO PARENTS AND EDUCATORS:
The understanding of any language begins with the acquisition of vocabulary, whether the language is spoken or manual. The books in the Talking Hands series provide readers, both young and old, with a first introduction to basic American Sign Language signs. Combining close photocues and simple, but detailed, line illustrations, children and adults alike can begin the process of learning American Sign Language. Let these books be an introduction to the world of American Sign Language. Most languages have regional dialects and multiple ways of expressing the same thought. This is also true for sign language. We have attempted to use the most common version of the signs for the words in this series. As with any language, the best way to learn is to be taught in person by a frequent user. It is our hope that this series will pique your interest in sign language.

Apple

There are 7,500 different types of apples in the world.

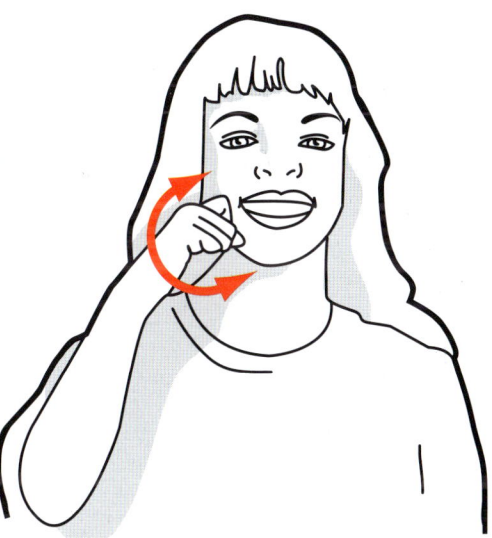

Make a fist and put the knuckle of your index finger against your cheek. Twist your wrist back and forth.

Banana

Motion as if you are peeling a banana.

> Banana plants are not trees—they are a kind of herb.

You can eat every part of a watermelon, even the seeds!

Watermelon

Make the "W" sign and touch it to your lips. Then thump your other wrist as if you are thumping a melon.

Orange

Make the "C" sign and then the "S" sign in front of your mouth twice.

The sign for orange—the color and the fruit—are the same!

Strawberry

Another sign for "strawberry" twists curved fingers at the end of an index finger.

Pinch two fingers and cup your hand in front of your face. Then twist and move downward.

Tomato

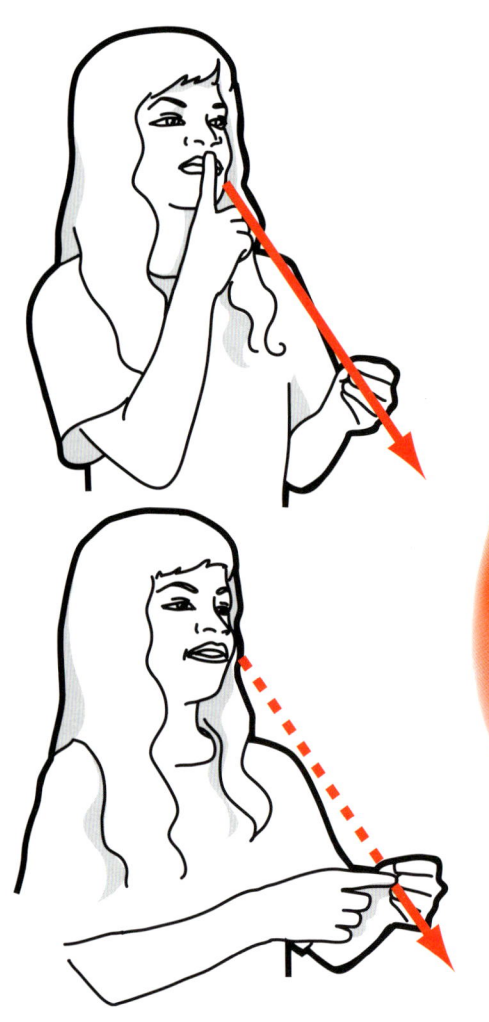

Flick your lips with your finger. Then motion as if you are slicing a tomato.

The biggest tomato in the world weighed over 7 pounds (3 kg)!

Corn

Corn is actually part of the grass family.

With your finger, motion as if you are eating a cob of corn, twisting and moving the cob right to left.

Hamburger

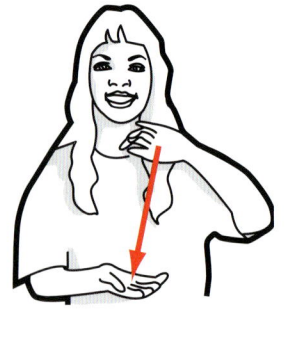 
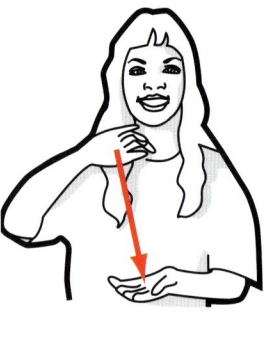 

Cup your right hand over your left. Clap them together softly. Then switch. Motion like you are making a "patty" with your hands.

Americans eat about 14 billion hamburgers a year.

Hot Dog

Hot dogs are also called "frankfurters" or "franks."

Make two "C" shapes together. Move your hands apart a bit, and make two fists. Make the "C" shapes again, then move your hands apart even more and make two fists.

Chicken

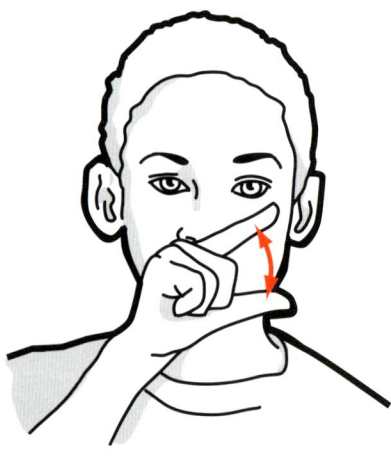

Open and close your fingers like a chicken's beak.

This sign for "chicken" can also be the sign for "bird."

The average person eats about 170 eggs a year!

Egg

Make the "H" sign with both hands. Tap your fingers together, then move down, as if you are breaking an egg.

Fish

Wiggle your hand and move it forward like a fish swimming along.

Trout is a popular type of fish to eat.

Lobster

A lobster's body does not have any bones.

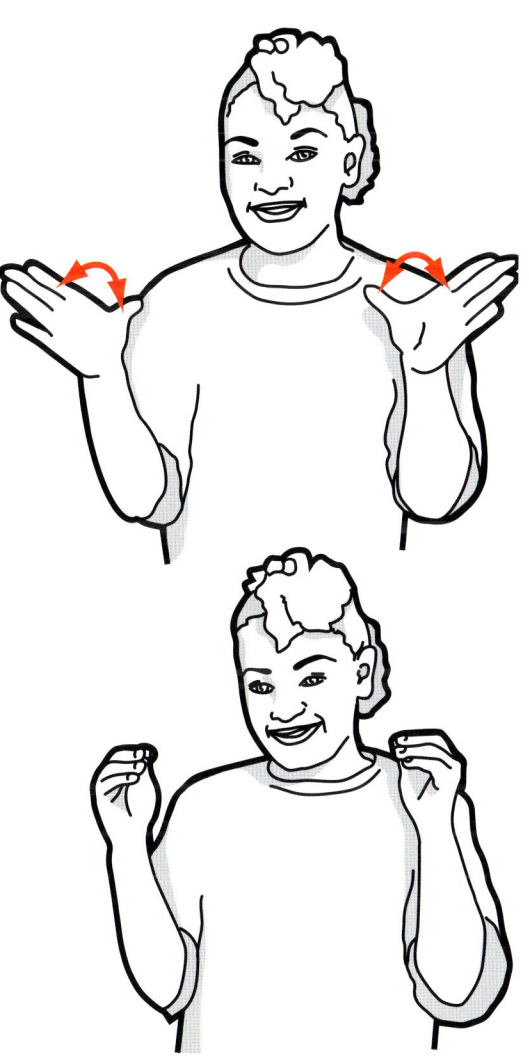

Open and close your hands like a lobster's claws.

Soup

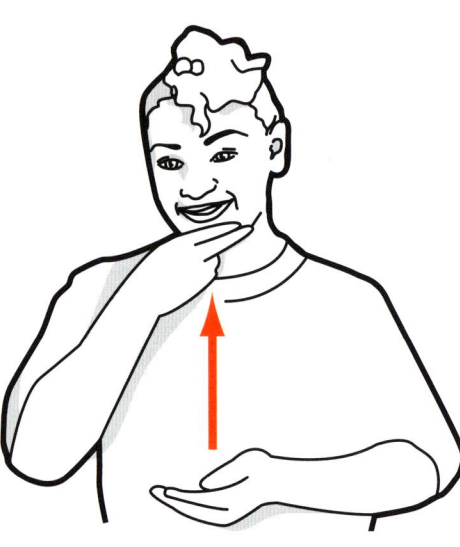

Cup one hand like a bowl. Use two fingers of your other hand to scoop toward your mouth.

Chicken-noodle soup is one of most popular types of soup.

Bread

Scientists think people have been eating bread for more than 10,000 years.

Your left hand stays still.
Curl your right hand slightly
and motion as if you are slicing bread.

Coffee

Make two fists and put them on top of each other. Keep the bottom hand still and make a small circle with your top hand.

The sign for "coffee" is like using an old-fashioned coffee grinder.

Milk

Most milk comes from cows. We also get milk from sheep, goats, and even buffalo.

Make the "C" sign. Then make the "S" sign. Repeat.

19

Pie

Pretend to "slice" two pieces of pie on one of your hands.

Cherry, apple, and pumpkin are all popular pie flavors.

Ice Cream

Americans eat about 20 quarts (almost 19 liters) of ice cream a year!

Make a fist and move it in front of your mouth as if you were licking an ice cream cone.

Chocolate

One hand is palm-side down.
The top hand makes the "C" sign.
Make two circles with your top hand,
as if you are stirring chocolate.

Just smelling chocolate can make people feel relaxed.

Cookie

People have been making cookies for over 2,000 years.

Make a loose "C" shape. Bring it down onto your other hand. Bring it up and put it down again, as if you are cutting out cookies.

A SPECIAL THANK YOU!

A special thank you to our models from the Program for Children Who are Deaf and Hard of Hearing at the Alexander Graham Bell Elementary School in Chicago, Illinois.

Aroosa loves reading and playing with her sister Aamna. Aroosa's favorite color is red.

Carla enjoys art, as well as all kinds of sports.

Deandre likes playing football and watching NFL games on television.

Destiny enjoys music and dancing. She especially likes learning new things.

Xiomara loves fashion, clothes, and jewelry. She also enjoys music and dancing.

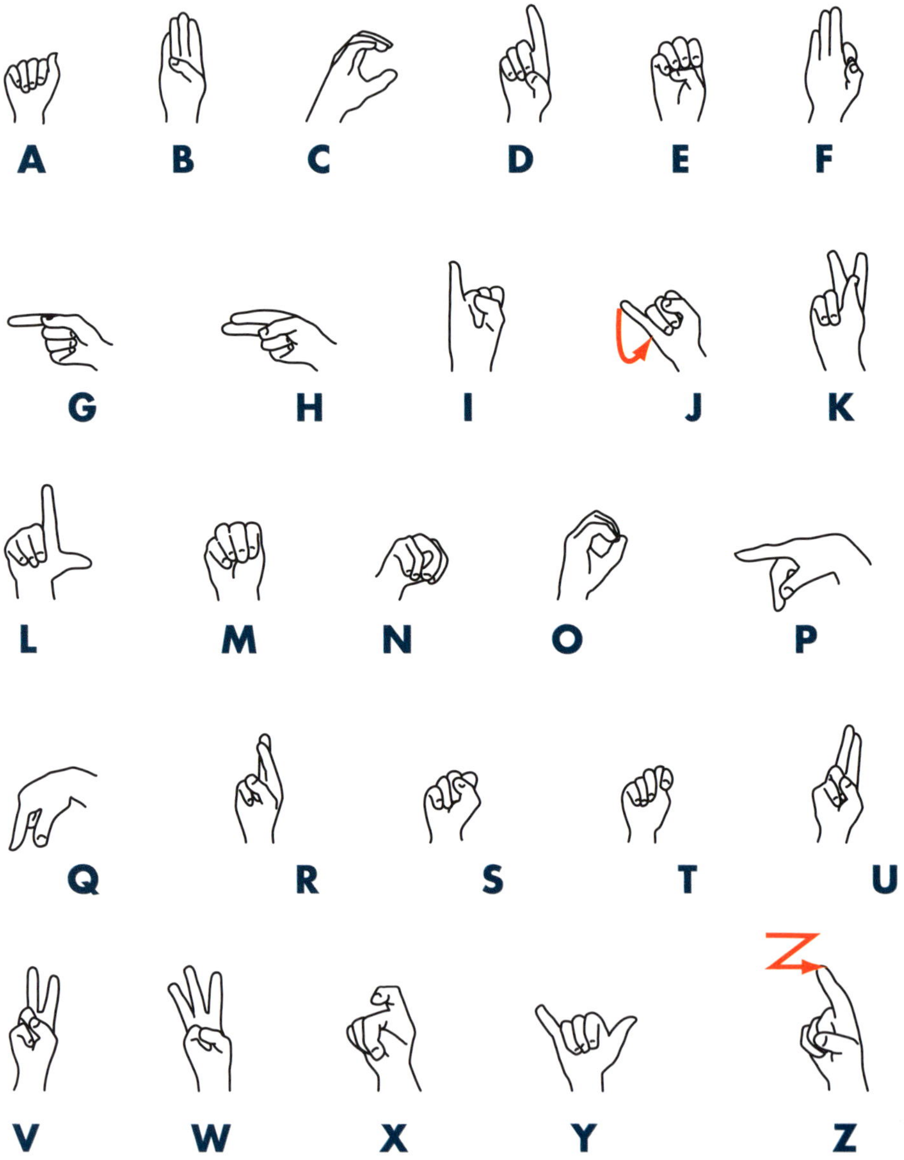